Conten

D1050391

Handbook For Sponsors

Authors:
Kathy Brown • Bob Duggan
Carol Gura • Rita Ferrone
Gael Gensler • Steve Lanza
Donna Steffen

Product Manager:
Maureen Kelly

Editor:
Karen Griffith

Book Design:
Barbara Mueller

Cover Design:
Karen McDonald

Nihil Obstat
Reverend George Smiga
Censor Librorum

Imprimatur
† *Most Reverend Anthony Pilla*
Bishop of Cleveland

July 8, 1997

The Nihil Obstat and Imprimatur are official declarations that the material reviewed is free of doctrinal or moral error. No implication is contained therein that those granting the Nihil Obstat and Imprimatur agree with the contents, opinions, or statements expressed.

Send all inquiries to:
RCL • Resources for Christian Living
200 Bethany Drive
Allen, Texas 75002-3804

Toll free   800-822-6701
Fax   800-688-8356

Printed in the United States of America

12700   ISBN 0-7829-0754-7
1 2 3 4 5   01 00 99 98 97

Welcome!

Thank you for responding to the invitation to be a sponsor. This is a very important ministry in the Church today. As a sponsor you accompany someone who is preparing to become a Catholic. You represent the parish community as you introduce the person to the Catholic way of life.

This booklet is designed to assist you in your ministry by giving you a brief description of the process of initiation in our Church today, focusing on the gifts you may bring to the ministry, and offering some practical suggestions on what to do (and what not to do!) while being a sponsor.

In the past many people who have served as sponsors have discovered this ministry to be a very powerful experience of faith and of the Church as community. May your experience as a sponsor be rewarding and a renewal of your faith!

UNDERSTANDING THE PROCESS

In the Catholic Church, accompanying someone on their journey of initiation is like the birthing of a child. As they learn what it means to be Catholic and discover the rich tradition of our Church, they awaken to a new way of living life. Your role is to be a companion; your task is to walk with them, guiding them through the process of the Church toward full initiation.

The official ministry of a sponsor begins when the companion you are sponsoring enters into a time of pastoral formation, called the Period of the Catechumenate. This period can extend for several months or several years, depending on the journey of your companion. Your first official act as a sponsor will be to introduce, and witness on behalf of, your inquirer at the Rite of Acceptance.

Your unofficial role may begin during the period of the Inquiry, or Pre–catechumenate. Parishes vary in when they assign sponsors. You may sponsor someone who has never been baptized. This person is called a catechumen. Or you may be a sponsor for a candidate, a person who was baptized in another Christian tradition or who was baptized Catholic but never received any formation in the Church.

The Church takes initiation very seriously in its desire to be faithful to the Gospel and to the Tradition of the Church. The Rite of Christian Initiation of Adults contains the official rituals and prayers of the Church for its catechumens and candidates. It is this rite that is used throughout the Roman Catholic Church.

As is evident in the Rite, the Church is aware that it takes time for people to grow in their faith and to understand the implications of the Gospel for daily life. The Church desires to respect the movement of the Holy Spirit in each person's life. During a gradual process of initiation a person grows in knowledge of the teachings of the Church, explores the meaning of the Scriptures for daily life, develops friendships with members of the parish community, learns to pray and worship in the Catholic tradition, and discovers the joy of serving others.

Throughout the entire process, the Church surrounds the catechumens and candidates with a loving community of support, care, and prayers. From the time they enter the catechumenate until their full initiation, the Church celebrates rites marking the moments of growth in faith and commitment. These public rites and rituals are usually celebrated in the midst of the parish community in the context of the Sunday liturgy.

At the time of initiation a catechumen celebrates the three sacraments of initiation: Baptism, Confirmation, Eucharist. A candidate is not rebaptized, but is initiated through a profession of faith, Confirmation, and Eucharist.

After initiation, the Church, especially through your ministry, continues to care for the newly initiated Catholics during the Period of Mystagogy. Hopefully the relationship that developed during the entire process of initiation continues far into the future . . . as fellow members in the Catholic Christian community!

The pages that follow give you some basic directives to help you fulfill your responsibilities as a sponsor and use the personal gifts you bring that will make your ministry successful.

Offer a Welcoming Spirit

"*When I came to the parish for the first time with my husband I was very apprehensive. He had been away from the Church for years and I was not Catholic. When I decided to become Catholic, I was so grateful for Sarah, my sponsor. I don't think I have ever experienced such welcome. She must have introduced me to fifty people that Sunday when we celebrated the Rite of Welcome. I certainly did feel welcome!*"

Jenny Wright

For Reflection:

▦ Have you ever moved to a new place, a new parish, a new job, a new neighborhood, a new city?

▦ Was there someone special who welcomed you?

▦ Describe your experience and how it felt.

$\mathcal{M}$any of the people who are becoming Catholic may also be new to the parish. They may not know anyone and sometimes it can be difficult to meet people. As a sponsor, you have many opportunities to introduce the catechumen or candidate to other people in the parish through simple practices of inviting your companion to join you at liturgy, at parish meetings, and at other events.

Being a sponsor is like being a bridge for a catechumen or candidate into the life of the parish. Even though the entire parish community has the responsibility to initiate new members, you, as the sponsor have the most direct opportunity to offer welcome and hospitality to the catechumen or candidate. What may seem like second nature to you, like what you do when you enter the Church, may be very strange and anxiety producing to your companion. Look for opportunities to familiarize your companion to the everyday rituals and etiquette of your parish. Listen for questions your companion asks about parish life and help him or her find the answer. Remember, simple actions, concrete responses, and explanations of how to do things all express welcome.

Practical Suggestions:

⊛ Invite your catechumen or candidate, along with your companion's family, to sit with you during the liturgy.

⊛ Introduce your family and your friends to your companion.

⊛ When you see your catechumen or candidate, smile and acknowledge his or her presence.

⊛ Call your companion by name!

⊛ Go through the parish bulletin with your companion and explain what the various activities listed are about.

⊛ Introduce your companion to some of the people whose names are in the bulletin.

⊛ Take your companion on a walk around the parish grounds or plant. Familiarize your companion with where things are and what activities take place there.

⊛ Actively respond to questions your companion asks about the Church or parish life.

Share Catholic Traditions

"*One of the things that attracted me to the Catholic Church was all of the ritual. Whenever I would enter a Catholic Church I felt as though I was entering into a very holy place. Now that I'm Catholic, I know I was right. I love all of the rituals and traditions. I really have to thank John, my sponsor, because he's the one who helped me to understand Catholic traditions and prayers.*"

James Morton

For Reflection:

▦ As a Catholic, who are the people who were most important in passing on the Catholic traditions to you?

▦ How did they pass on the traditions?

▦ Which Catholic traditions are the most important to you today?

▦ Who are the most important saints for you?

*C*atholicism has a very rich tradition. The centuries have provided us with a vast array of ways to ponder the mystery of God. Saints, relics, rosaries, smells, bells, and symbols—all contribute to the beauty and drama of the life of the Catholic Church. Cathedrals, shrines, basilicas, convents, and monasteries are places rich in tradition and history that can provide an opportunity to learn about our faith. The variety of prayers of the Church enhances the faith life of Catholics. A gift that you can bring as a sponsor is to help your candidate or catechumen understand our Catholic traditions.

Sharing Church traditions will help your catechumen or candidate discover the ways our faith is lived and brought into the home throughout the year. When we think about it, we begin to realize that these simple practices, traditions, and prayers from our treasury provide the environment for our Catholic faith to grow. As a guide into this treasury, you bring to the catechumen or candidate the gift of our entire Tradition.

If you are unsure about the meaning of some of the Church's practices and traditions, there are many resources available to assist you. (See references.) You should also feel free to consult the initiation team, parish staff, or clergy as sources for material and information. And don't be surprised if you don't know the answer to some questions. It is okay to say, "I don't know, but I'll find out!" This is a great time for you and your catechumen or candidate to discover our Tradition together.

Remember one thing: You are part of the living Tradition of the Church. It is your faith and your experiences that God uses to pass the faith to your companion.

Practical Suggestions:

⊛ With your catechumen or candidate visit the cathedral, a local shrine, a basilica, or any place in the diocese that would be interesting for someone learning about becoming Catholic.

⊛ Share what roles statues, candles, holy water, holy cards, or any other Catholic items have in our Catholic tradition.

⊛ Explain the meanings of seasonal activities such as the creche, the Advent wreath, ashes, blessed palms.

⊛ Tell stories of the Church's saints, stressing why and how we venerate them.

⊛ Teach the prayers and the way of the rosary.

⊛ Introduce the Liturgy of the Hours.

⊛ Pray the Stations of the Cross or the Way of the Cross together.

⊛ Share the traditional prayers of the Church.

⊛ Take part in Sunday Mass together.

⊛ Share childhood memories of growing up Catholic and share some of the ways your family participated in the traditions of the Church.

Listen

"*Learning to be quiet and just listen to Sharon [catechumen] was the most difficult part of my role as a sponsor. I was so used to telling other people how they should live their lives; now I had to learn to be quiet and listen in a new way, without trying to give unasked-for advice. I think I grew more from learning to listen than anything else I did as a sponsor. I must say that my friends and husband sure appreciated my new way of listening, too!*"

Lydia Kane

For Reflection:

 To whom do you go when you really want someone to listen to you?

 What makes that person a good listener?

 What are your strengths as a listener?
Your weaknesses?

$\mathcal{L}$istening is a gift we can give to one another. It is an art; not everyone is a good listener. Yet, this skill is essential for a sponsor. As the catechumens and candidates explore the Scriptures, their lives will be challenged by the demands of the Gospel. Reflecting on the teachings of the Church with you will challenge their values and perceptions of the world. In addition, their past hurts and pains may surface during times of reflection and sharing. Therefore, providing opportunities for your companion to share what is going on in his or her life is critical. Equally important is having you there to listen.

Perhaps the greatest gift you as a sponsor can offer is to listen with reverence and respect. Your ability to listen acknowledges and affirms God's active presence in your companion's life. Listening conveys that you believe the life of your catechumen or candidate is a valuable source for God's communication. By listening, you proclaim your trust in the power of the Gospel to transform lives.

Sometimes when a catechumen or candidate asks a question, there is a deeper question lying underneath the one asked. Usually this is a question that a person is not totally comfortable asking. As a good listener, you need to listen for the deeper, hidden question, tacitly giving your companion freedom to raise the deeper issue that the unspoken question addresses.

A good listener does not probe or push others to reveal more than they desire to reveal at the moment. Our task as listeners is to create an environment which is safe and comfortable. We do this by allowing catechumens and candidates to share only what they feel comfortable sharing. By not probing or pushing, we build trust.

Practical Suggestions:

- Pay attention to what your companion is saying instead of trying to figure out what to say before he or she finishes speaking.

- Do not try to repair your companion's life. Instead, offer support, which communicates respect for your companion and generates belief in his or her ability to solve life problems.

- Listen confidentially, without judging your companion.

- After each meeting, make it a point to ask how your companion experienced the session and if there are any questions.

- Pay attention to what your companion is *not* saying.

Share Life and Share Faith

"*When Ray was laid off, we didn't know what we were going to do. Financially it was all we could do to keep the children in the parish school. I called my sponsor and told her we were going to put off becoming Catholic for right now. I told her that my husband and I felt we needed to get our lives together before we would be accepted as Catholics. My sponsor laughed and said to me, 'Do you think you have to be a perfect, happy family before you are accepted by us? Now is the time we need each other. Stay with us and we will be strong together.' I learned more about what it means to be Catholic during that time than I did in all of the previous sessions together. Thank God, we stayed.*"

Mary Beth Snider

For Reflection:

In your life who are the people that have influenced you the most by their living the faith?

Why do you say this?

List three reasons why you love the Church.

What helps you talk about your faith to others?

$\mathcal{B}$ecoming a Catholic is not only about learning what Catholics believe. It is also about discovering how Catholics take what they believe and live it in their daily lives. Seeing leads to believing. By coming to know you, your family, and your way of life, your catechumen or candidate is offered an insight into how Catholics take the Gospel and the teachings of the Church and attempt to live their faith. By sharing your life, you model what it means to live faith.

A willingness to share your lived faith is an essential dimension of being a sponsor. It helps your catechumen or candidate to hear how you have grown in your faith, to know that you still struggle and have questions about life, and to understand the values you bring to decision making. It is helpful to your companion to hear from you about concrete experiences in your life where your faith has made a difference. Include both the joys and struggles you have experienced on your faith journey. It is important to communicate that a person does not have to be perfect in order to become a Catholic.

Sharing your life and faith takes time. You will need time to talk, to do activities together, and to take part in the functions related to the catechumenate.

Throughout the process of initiation, remember that your life communicates how God's presence comes into ordinary living and makes it extraordinary. You are the witness of the great mystery of God's transforming love. As a sponsor, you have the privilege of not only giving witness but also being a privileged witness to the mystery of God's movement in the catechumen or candidate's life.

Practical Suggestions:

⚛ Faithfully take part in the initiation sessions with your catechumen or candidate.

⚛ Participate in initiation retreats with your catechumen or candidate.

⚛ Invite your catechumen or candidate to parish activities such as parties, festivals, fish fries, retreats, benefits, or other special events.

⚛ Take part in diocesan events such as concerts, conferences, or prayer services with your catechumen or candidate.

⚛ Share childhood memories of your faith.

⚛ Extend an invitation to join you and your family for dinner.

⚛ Make contact at least once a week with your catechumen or candidate.

⚛ Get together after Mass or some other time during the week.

⚛ Share your everyday questions, joys, pains, and happiness.

⚛ Share your faith.

Introduce Ministry

"One night my sponsor invited me to join him at the soup kitchen. I dreaded going. I have always figured homeless people could get a job if they wanted to. But that night the homeless issue hit a little close to home. Business was bad and my family and I were living on the financial edge. That night I realized that I could be homeless too. Meeting some of the homeless people, listening to the Scriptures, and learning about the Catholic Church's tradition of care for the poor really helped me. I'm still financially on the edge, but through the help of my sponsor, I am learning to trust in God more and to be a lot more compassionate toward those who are less fortunate than I am."

Joe Hernandez

For Reflection:

 List as many of the experiences you have had over your lifetime of being of service to others.

 What did you find most satisfying?

 How do you hear yourself being called to service today?

 What are the major areas of service your parish is involved in?

Catholics have a great tradition of helping people. In the history of the Church, Catholics have cared for the sick, provided shelter and food for the poor, defended those on the margins of society, and so much more. This outreach of service to others is an essential aspect of the mission of the Church. Many parishes today continue to serve people who are homeless, sick, or hurting. Parish social ministries provide the setting for sharing and acting on the Church's mission.

As disciples of Jesus Christ, we are called to participate in the mission of the Church through our service to others. It is during the Period of the Catechumenate that you will introduce your catechumen or candidate to the different parish social ministries. Through a process of discernment, your catechumen or candidate may decide to volunteer in one of the social ministries.

As a sponsor, you can assist your catechumen or candidate. First, you can find out what social ministries the parish or diocese is involved in. Some parishes have volunteers who visit the sick or the homebound, or who help out at soup kitchens or local shelters. Other parishes are involved in larger community action projects in their neighborhoods and cities. The diocese may have a legislative network for people to join.

Second, as a sponsor you can help connect your catechumen or candidate with volunteers who are involved in the various parish or diocesan social ministries. These volunteers introduce the ministry by inviting the catechumen or candidate to come and see what they do, and by sharing what the ministry means for them and for the Church. The purpose of these experiences is not to recruit volunteers. Rather, it is to enlighten the catechumen or candidate on some of the ways Catholics put their faith into action.

Practical Suggestions:

- Research the social ministries offered in your parish or diocese.

- Invite your catechumen or candidate to join parishioners at a local soup kitchen or shelter.

- Accompany the minister of the sick who brings Holy Communion to the homebound or those in the hospital.

- Attend parish or diocesan programs concerned with social justice issues.

- Invite your catechumen or candidate to participate in special seasonal projects, such as adopting a family during the Christmas season, collecting food at Thanksgiving, or giving money to the Rice Bowl during Lent.

- Go Christmas caroling at a local senior citizen center.

- Join together with other parishes working on community service projects.

- Share how your living out the social values of the Gospel impacts your understanding of the mission of the Church.

Offer Friendship

"*When the director told me just to be a friend to my companion, I found that it was not as easy as it sounded. I realized that being a spiritual companion is different from other types of friendships. I don't think I have ever before had a friend to talk with about God, about my faith, or about the Church. I learned a lot about being a friend, and I hope that it has helped me to be a better friend to others.*"

Miles Nash

For Reflection:

▨ Describe the qualities of your best friends.

▨ How would you describe yourself as a friend?

▨ What are the most important benefits to you of other people's friendship?

▨ What do you see as the costs of being a friend?

$\mathcal{P}$robably no greater gift exists than the gift of friendship. As a sponsor what does it mean to you to offer friendship? The qualities of friendship offered by a sponsor should share various characteristics with the other friendships in our lives. Long-lasting friendships usually are the result of a shared history with one another or of the gradual discovery of each other's similar values or interests. Friendships take time and are built by good communication of who we are and what we believe in.

The type of friendship a sponsor offers includes a welcoming presence, an enthusiasm to guide the catechumen or candidate into the parish life, and a willingness to listen to the life experiences and the journey of another person. It also includes a desire to share one's life, to share one's friends and family, and to share one's faith. This is a unique friendship built upon a faith relationship.

Some sponsors develop deep and long lasting friendships with their companions. Others have good relationships that are not as deep or long lasting but are very beneficial to the catechumen or candidate during the process. Sometimes the relationship between a sponsor and a catechumen or candidate does not work out. This happens for different reasons and does not mean you as a sponsor failed. If it happens, it is the responsibility of the initiation coordinator and you to recognize that the catechumen or candidate would be better served by a new sponsor.

Ultimately friendship is a gift. Be open to the possibility of receiving the gift of a new friend.

Practical Suggestions:

⚜ Take the initiative to reach out to your catechumen or candidate.

⚜ Be consistent and faithful in your attention to the catechumen or candidate.

⚜ Listen.

⚜ Share your life and your faith.

⚜ Be honest.

⚜ Admit it if the relationship is not working.

Witness

"*When I was first told that I would have to stand up in front of the parish and talk about my candidate, I thought the director was nuts! I am so shy—or so I thought! When the time came, Father Mike had to ask me to 'wrap up' what I had to say. I guess when I got started I realized I had a lot to say about Margaret. She was wonderful and had gone through such a tremendous change. When I think back about my role as sponsor, I think I am just now becoming aware of what a privilege and honor it was for me. I now realize the role of the sponsor is so incredibly important and a very powerful experience of how God works through all of us. I was truly blessed.*"

Linda Manning

For Reflection:

☒ Have you ever had the experience of speaking on someone's behalf or of hearing someone speak on your behalf?

☒ What is a credible witness?

☒ Describe your experience and how it felt.

*I*n the early Church, people who wanted to become Christians were sponsored by members of the community. The sponsor would help the person understand what it meant to live as a Christian by being a witness in his or her own life and by guiding the catechumen during the preparation period.

Becoming a Christian in the early Church could be very risky, not only for the catechumen but also for the community. It was important to know the authenticity of his or her commitment to Christianity. The sponsor was expected to vouch for the catechumen's sincerity and to give witness to the community on behalf of the catechumen.

Today we do not fear being persecuted for our faith in Jesus Christ. We are not on the lookout for people who are infiltrating the Church so they can report us to the authorities. However, it is still important for the Church to help catechumens and candidates discern the meaning of committing themselves to living the Gospel. As a sponsor you assist your catechumen or candidate in this discernment process. Through your example you witness to the commitment of living the faith.

The Church has a special responsibility to discern the commitment of your catechumen or candidate. Therefore, the Church's immediate contact is through you. Periodically you will be asked if your catechumen or candidate is listening and responding to God's word, and if he or she is sharing the company of other Catholic Christians by joining us in prayer or in the apostolic life. As a sponsor you are the symbol of the Church's care and concern for the catechumen or candidate, and you are responsible to witness to the rest of the Church on their faith journey.

As you enter into this ministry it might seem like an overwhelming responsibility to care for another person. That is why it is important for you to know that you do not perform this ministry alone. God, in Christ Jesus, and through the power of the Holy Spirit, goes before you, preparing the way. Trust in God's love for you and your catechumen or candidate. Above everything else, enjoy the blessings that come through the ministry of sponsor.

Practical Suggestions:

- Periodically ask your catechumen or candidate how they feel they are progressing.

- Assist in preparing your catechumen or candidate for the rites.

- Take time to listen to your catechumen or candidate's fears or anxieties about becoming a Catholic.

- Affirm growth and change in your catechumen or candidate as you observe these.

- Attend the rehearsals for the rites.

- Participate in the rites and be prepared for witness.

Suggested Resources

Catechism of the Catholic Church. Allen, Texas: Thomas More, 1994.

Deedy, John. *The Catholic Fact Book*. Allen, Texas: Thomas More, 1986.

Dues, Greg. *Catholic Customs and Traditions: A Popular Guide*. Connecticut: Twenty-third Publications, 1994.

Foy, Felician and Avato Rose, ed. *Catholic Almanac*. Huntington, Indiana: Our Sunday Visitor.

Lewinski, Ron. *Guide for Sponsors*. Chicago: Liturgy Training Publication, 1993.

Morris, Thomas H. *Walking Together in Faith*. New York: Paulist Press, 1992.